Joyriding Down Utopia Avenue

b

SIMON FRENCH

JOYRIDING DOWN UTOPIA AVENUE

Coverstory books

First published in paperback format by Coverstory
books, 2021

This second edition published in paperback format by
Coverstory books, 2025

ISBN 978-1-0686701-3-8

www.coverstorybooks.com

Also by Simon French:

The Deadwing Generation
(Coverstory Books, 2022 & 2025)

Contents

❄

Bedwetter Stays at The Savoy

A weekend
for his eyes to skate down a frozen Thames,

on the lookout for John Rennie's London Bridge,
take a stroll

through gunpowdered Parliament
as the tour guide recommends.

Scarcely time to sip tea before being whisked
to the Crystal Palace

dragging its light across the sky,
empty of Luftwaffe; they're due to appear

in tonight's spectacular
with WestEnders scurrying for the Underground.

Afterwards his taxi staggers
through drunkards, past street corner migrants

before nosing-up at The Savoy.
A king-size bed coaxes him to sleep,

delivers him to the breakfast table
while the maid recoils

to find he'd been drowning all night
in the waters of a melted river.

Timebond

Warmed by your blood
I always have time for you
as constantly
you lavish attention on my face.
If I tire you push me on.
If I speed you apply brakes,
such is your care.

I know your eye roves,
occasionally glancing
at a brazenly chiming voice
or a digital wink
but it's me at night by your side,
that watches over you,
and in the morning
over coffee, offers time
before trains, buses, meetings.

You keep me dry,
you wind me up,
you keep me on my tocks.
I'm fit to turn,
your very own Greenwich lean time
in black and gold.
I've got to hand it to you,
our love is numeric,
so unconditional
that we don't even give it
a second thought.

Together They Water Begonias

his hose from the outside tap,
hers curling from the uPVC kitchen window
and in patio-lantern light
hoses crisscross, writhing
like snakes in passion.

Borders gulp
with the generosity of their shower
while laughter alerts neighbours
who peer through pinched curtains
at the naked gardeners.

Must have been on the vino
the neighbours will later concur,
but for now they tut back to their pillows,
missing the chase-around, the soaking
across a charred lawn.

Wet skin embraces by the rockery;
a kiss under the pinprick sky
whose rain seems to have forgotten
how to fall like the confetti
that monsooned some sixty years ago.

Javelin

Hey Olympian!
I was so impressed –
in your apartment,
those strong arms,
the trophied shelves of excellence.

I was your secret relief,
in the grip of your voice I stripped
and you pushed me to the carpet,
rolled me onto my front,
tracksuit bottoms around your ankles.
Your weight took my breath away.

Felt a moist meat prodding
so I clenched with the power of a victory fist
as you pounded into the virgin turf of me
and ludicrously I wondered
what Mum and Dad were watching on tv,
A Question Of Sport?

I bit the pain of those minutes,
felt you seep into me.
Trying to sound cool,
Can I go home now?

And so to here, right now,
having forgotten you Olympian
and in Carl's gym-slogged arms
somehow stuck unnoticed,
a javelin stirs the ghostwound

so politely Carl, not tonight Carl,
can't cope Carl, give you a call Carl.

Like a re-run through a misted camera
it all came back to me,
from your apartment,
retching, running
and not knowing where to go,
how to stop.

A Day for the Shakers

White-timbered homesteads.
A bell punctuates the day,
informs of meals,
nudges leather-shoed feet
into a plain step to God.

New Hampshire trees in surround,
and when the apple is keen
womenfolk set hands to work
making sauce
for singing tongues.

Children hang their coats
on the pegboard,
learn easy-stepped dances
on the outer edge of Heaven.

Men labour over maplewood or hickory,
sawing, carving out stark creations,
their fingers and thumbs like the wood,
stained ochre and red.

When the moon takes up residence
and all work is done,
to sit and know the chair holds;
that is enough.

Remains of a Cheapskate

sit seething at the wifely extravagance. His eyes
flinch over bank statements. He whose heart

dances with vouchers,
fingers the calculator to within an inch of its life.

He'll never drag a valentine from his wallet
to fund an unexpected throng of roses
to come knocking,

her *surprise*

from his trawl through the chilly aisles —
a microwave dinner
gasping on its use-by date.

He's nailed the pence of every turning kilowatt;
daughter in the upstairs dark,
not daring to deploy her bedside light.

The remains of a cheapskate are to be found
buried in brazen-holed jumpers and socks,

a jumble to step over on the way out.

Picasso's Armies

You prowl
in woodland idyll
trampling fern & bluebell,
camouflaged,
splattgunning
in undergrowth;
it's an abstract war
so with a Magritte of the teeth
you take a hit,
snipered
by paintball after paintball
exploding multicoloured blood,
your bruises abound
so don't dilly-Dali
make a dash for cover,
cower in the secrecy of thickets
while your team
accomplish their mission,
gloss over your AWOL
& exit one & all,
a load of Pollocks,
bravery;
every man fully decorated.

Winter's Lucky Lady

The bingo dreams of Vera
keep her lumbering every Saturday night
in plastic rainhood through cloudburst & wind.

Her cleaners' knee clicks the ache
up steps, the last suck on a Richmond;
her Hippodrome of chance a warm glow of light & noise.

That same seat creaks
under the weight of her Mablethorpe reverie;
a caravan, local chippie, it's a week away from bucket & mop.

Come on Caller
let some numbers loose, the silenced tables hang
on your every banter, quick fingers twitch in wait for *Duck & Dive*

or *Heaven's Gate 78*;
the winner's whoop sends shockwaves to the gods
leaving Vera to deflate in taxi, an echo of bleach growing louder & harsh.

By the Short and Curlies

There's an Eastbourne on his mind
with these greying-hair days
as another birthday sticks the bungalow
deep in his heart's dread.
He's an inkling of the coming years,
that he'll start to enjoy sparrows, robins,
hanker for peonies, smile
as kittens tumble on the lawn;
things that in his teen days as now,
would only get his tedium's top award.
Punked-up back in the 70's,
Barnet's finest spit 'n' anger merchant
sanded down over years,
the varnish of a married stretch,
keenly motor-trading with an eye for the bodywork.
Now he tweezers out
those pubic ghosts
that hint of a certain coastal town
where every attic chokes
on decommissioned dreams, regrets
and from the comfy chair
a laughter flutes across the garden
as Tabby stalks for the kill.

The Courthouse Steps

Police boots clump up Courthouse steps,
overtake leather shoes
burdened under the weight of justice,
freshly plucked from His Honour's shoe-tree
as morning rears its villains to the dock.

Prada heels clipclop the Clerk of the Court across marble
and into a nifty sidestep
around the mooching moccasins of Witness Liaison
in conference with Hush Puppied Probation Officer,
feet a pre-trial fidget.

Pinstriped legs with well-mannered brogues
pass the time of litigation opposite the Versace heels
of a Solicitor besieged with files.
Meanwhile a Stenographer shuffles coffee-stained mules
along to Court 2.

The jury foreman gets to his loafers

On the Courthouse steps a flip-flopped girl
sees Nikes leap into the prison van,
blows kisses to a blacked-out window.
Child waves to daddy. Barefoot.

I'm Back on the Honey Conchita

the only sweetness
in a mouth full of bullets and bile

hideawhile
under a nonchalant sun

shack seems empty without you
looking out across the airfield

afternoon limps along
slow as an ageing cockroach

glassless window
welcomes in the buzzing of the peninsula

dzidzilche flowers, tajonal flowers
smell like you did

that night in the motel
before the grubby linen suit

got cute, nailed our alias to the wall
and snatched you back

   hasta luego amigo

mockingbird in the red oleander bush
i swear i'll shoot his song into a mission grave

so whenever's the day i'll hear your voice again
tempting bees to your lips

i'm back on the honey Conchita

Angel of the Northbound

You like to park up
in derelict petrol stations
to keep an eye on the traffic

or wait on some motorway bridge,
looking down
as partially tethered tarpaulin
flaps hysterically around a lorry's timber run,
as businessmen in coolcut suits and loose ties
yawn deep into their dashboards

because maybe one day
you'll be needed,
after the pile-upping crush of metal,
to rescue a bloodied beauty,
to resuscitate the cradled head.

You stand illuminated
under the carpark lights of a Travelodge,
dream of earrings in the fast lane,

practise modesty
to imagined microphones, camera crews,
tell them how you squeezed her hand,
asked her name,
assured her everything was going to be okay.

The Curious World of the Nut Allergy

You were coy and fluttered once
when we chased those early dates
through the calendar, down our local,
kissing salt to each other
from the dry-roasted.
Rebounding together
off the tension of vows;
years building like the tiers of wedding cake
and mortgaged to the scalp
with our pristine home,
you've come out of your shell.
Little traces of you rash my lips
into sparring.
Your vanity consumes the bathroom.
You cluck out tasks.
A histamine rises in the throat.
The appetite now urging me
to take a nibble where the nut can't find.

Visiting Elizabeth Kershaw

Oil paintings of oceans hang on walls;
gilded wood frames
from which brush-stroked frigates

will never escape. We sit in the parlour
on shabby chintz. It's a trove of porcelain
and cobweb.

Dad follows Mrs. Kershaw
to the dripping bathroom tap, leaves me
to take cups and saucers to the kitchen.

I step into her garden.
There's a brazier bulging
with wings of half-burnt paper;

dots and squiggles, some Italian words.
Her husband
had been a little-known composer

and here the manuscripts of his lifetime,
left for wind and flame
to savour each last note.

The Cherries of Beaufays

A slight twist was all it took
to relieve the branches.
Each with our degrees of vertigo
I steadied on an untrusted rung,
turned my head to see a tractor
disappear into an afternoon air
filled with midges.

For the fruit,
ripe under an aching sun,
wicker baskets waltzed in a light wind,
hung on the crook of boughs
like handbags on old ladies' arms.
We filled them
with the juicy stock of our labours.

Your father's Citroen,
worn down on the kilometre of years,
yawned an open boot, awaited our harvest.
I heard your sister and her friend giggle
as they walked
alongside the outhouse wall.

I smiled as your eyes darted
into easy pickings around you.
Strained into the leafy interior
but just out of reach,
withdrew my hand, regained balance.

Hazeldene

There's a Lancaster Bomber on their fridge,
frozen in take-off.
She can't reach to dust there now
so he does between feeding and bathing her.

While she sleeps
or watches Bargain Hunt
from under the blanket on the sofa,
he'll busy himself with Airfix kits.

He's building a squadron;
the Kittyhawk, the de Havilland Mosquito,
aims them at the window.
Blobs of glue congeal on his fingers.

It's Mr. Shoemaker Travelling at 1,100mph

The fastest travelling ashes ever.
Wow Eugene!
Now you're a pioneer
in a NASA craft
looping the Moon in an urn.

The trajectory of your epitaph,
a hymn to calculus.
I bet you'd be real flattered,
you with eyes

that spied a bolting celestial rock
in the black and dazzle,
predicted its punch
into Jupiter.

Then crater hunting
along the Tanami Track, Alice Springs,
to suffer your own impact —

Car Crash.

So hurtle with the gravity of mourning
to a collision
with the Moon's south pole.
A cloud of exploding debris to settle
as your tribute in burnings,

leaving you one step closer
to the hand that bowls the comets.

His Great Outdoors

He was always bare-chested
from that moment in the year
when summer threatened to excite the mercury

till autumn began taking leaves.
My best friend's dad. A builder, balded early
and forever the ladies' man.

It's how I remember him.
Pitching a tent. Holidays
where he'd chase us round caravans.

Where he'd stand under a searing sky,
a golden giant of a man
who'd wade into the lake

and we'd follow.
Hands would secure us above water
until the fish in us took off alone.

Today his wife sits, talks of the melanomas,
slabs of skull they had to drill out
leaving potholes. Daily dressings.

Then misfiring neurons
and he was a young man again
diving off Arundel bridge,

swimming with the boys,
being dazzled by light,
losing sight of the jetty.

Old Town Fires

Lewes illuminated.
You're not sure of the year.
Clues are muffled by the woosh and boom
and as soon as you find a blown newspaper
along come crowds to trample the headlines,

cheering the procession. Then you recognise faces;
Thatcher and Reagan. So you're in the eighties, except
their faces are grotesque, with giant papier-mâchéd bodies.
Everyone jeers, taunts them. You join in,
demand they burn.

Breaking from the throng, you stop on the bridge.
Catch your breath. Look into the Ouse.
Faces stare up, a beautiful Polaroid boy,
a grey-haired woman with teeth missing,
a London actor from the swinging sixties, photographs

on the wrong side of the water, ebbing out of another time
as along the high street tar barrels are raced
by men in guernseys.
You swear you hear their voices *We won't be druv!*
This convinces you some great victory is being celebrated,

a freedom for England and a bonfire in every eye.
You find yourself offering prayers to protestant martyrs
but can't for the life of you recall their names.
The moon turns orange. Drums. A church bell
dawdles through gunpowder air. Your throat is dry.

You're lost but not scared.
At a firesite chanting spits, *Burn the Pope. Burn the Pope.*
Cheering as effigies singe. Blair, Bush. Bin Laden.
The year seeps into downland as flames rise.
A father hoists his son above the crowd. Mother gulps Pepsi.

You're in a foreign country, late autumn,
one minute in tunic or ruffs, the next denim or suede.
The hotel locks its doors at midnight
but you've no idea of time, date,
happy to look at all the faces. You don't notice the rockets,
it's the faces you'll not forget.

The Turn

You're wondering why,
what you'd done to deserve it, but for now
let's just say it was

because I could. It was the right moment,
you coming out of your house, off to work,
smelling of coffee

and your hand, at convenient height. The first bite,
wrapped around your little finger,
through to bone,

I really took you by surprise, snarling,
thrashing – boy was I good – tearing through
flesh, muscle, tendon, the red stuff everywhere

and once I get the taste. If it's any help,
you didn't look at me in a threatening way
or fail to offer an affectionate enough greeting.

You didn't encroach on my territory.
It's a duty to guard my garden,
the pavement is of no concern.

Can't tell me you don't understand.
You with that woman the other night
as you both shambled back from town.

You knew she wanted to go home
but there was that *moment*
to shunt her through your front door.

You'd make a great Staffie.

Missing Person

The day is stretched.
Passengers traipse from the steamer
along the jetty, they squint,

filter out to ice-cream sellers, gift shops,
passing the poster;
Have you seen this man?

His face,
leached by light,
stares out to yachts

dithering in Windermere heat.
Children gulp Fanta. Old ladies
melt onto benches. Leaflets fan.

Last seen wearing…
Japanese tourists snap at boathouses,
ducks.

…grey anorak, jeans and white trainers.
A Vespa snarls around the lake road,
into town, beeping a way through crowds

that haven't noticed the poster —
contact the Police if seen
as somewhere a wife, a mother, children

may imagine the day
they walk the waterfront
and find the poster gone,

replaced in the window
by snack prices
and departure times to the lake's other side.

Windfall

Mum has collected the apples
discarded by gravity

and placed them
in a wicker basket

resting now on the patio table,
waiting for an artist

and his puddles of oil.
She and I sit at the table in tired sunlight,

chat, sipping wine
against the backdrop

of Autumn dismantling the garden,
and her apples, punctured, a little bruised,

still offering their lustre, their sweet promise
to what's left of the day.

Weed

In this treacle of heat
where dog piss echoes its fume along the street

some reggae heartbeats from a ramshackle house.
Through an open window

she hears the song,
  make it legal, love it good.

Brings to mind her son, stashed in parka-jacket,
convinced God was hiding in every wheelie-bin

watching him. An apocalypse for one
and then for the many of him as he broke

into angry colours of himself. *Skinning-up,
smoking joints*, she hates those words.

Lost him to Council heights
and in the time it takes to sing the chorus

she replays the moment
he jumped

Homecoming

Lucas moves around the garden
showing how they'd stalk the Taliban,
it's almost *cartoon*,
the conjured-up ruins, the imagined gun
dispensing bullets.

On the barbecue steak begins its hiss and spit

Fist-size spiders, covert
in empty boots.
The faces of schoolgirls
opening books, the seduction of chalk
on board.
These are some of his stories.

Skewers are turning, smoke strays

Sounded like hell, the day
his best mate
chose the wrong piece of land
to offer weight to, a leg
flying past Lucas's head and later

they ate dates and chocolate
in memory
and no-one could find words.
Lucas ring-pulls a lager. Throw the grenade.
Throw the grenade.

Sweat from forehead drips onto spent briquettes, ash

Windchimes

Triumph convertible
aims for disabled parking -
it's the Ceausescus;
the sound of metatarsals
clatter across the Garden Centre car park.

Nicolae's patella is holed enough
for finches to squeeze through.
Elena runs phalanges
through oat grass.

They mull over gazebos,
consider a pond, koi,
but rule them out
as needing constant attention.
Nicolae tires

so they sip Darjeeling
in the cafe, tendrils of cartilage
hang from hipbones,
swing in the terrace breeze.
Treat themselves to carrot cake.

Linking bones,
careful to avoid the Virginia Creeper
only too keen
to thread its way around ribcages.
Nicolae ponders a rake – yes something

needs raking over.
Herbaceous perennials wow Elena.
They fumble for change,
saunter to the car

with no ears for the check-out girl shouting
you've not paid enough
the engine fires into life,
you still owe!

Italy Goes About Its Business

Meteo hot.
Along the jagged arc of the gulf of Napoli
scooters filter like coffee
through the parping trickle of *traffico*.

A hydrofoil unzips the sea
while children of fishermen
kick the *Azzurri* dream into a football.
Ripened women with seadrift hair
thread their needles,
chase waves from torn nets.

Aerials and crucifixes are staggered
along rooflines
of apartments flaking like pastries,
shutters open,
balconies with apparitions of laundry
gusting into a brief life.

Aerobica classes flex in a studio
where net curtains are tied back,
looking like trim-waisted brides
peeking from the window
at yuccas, bougainvillea,
at a businessman in Dolce & Gabbana's finest cut.

At the Lido Alimuri
a bather bakes.
After each breezy ruffle combs hair
back into a precision of quiff and wave.
Fingers plunge into moisturiser, butter face
before walking alongside girls
pretending not to notice.

Large *Americanos* in slacks, anoraks
order beer. *Prego*!
In a majolica-tiled terrace
between lemon groves,
tomorrow's trips are being planned
with Visuvio sulking under multiplying cloud;

Pompeii is next on the agenda.

Fieldnotes

Wind zipped through his brilliantined hair;
her open-top Bugatti, lipstick red,
sped them around walled cities

where widows would gasp
and boys chase into their afterdust.

They'd gust down streets of mudbrick,
she, the American, at the wheel, ray-banned
and headscarved against the Yemeni sun

and he, my father, pointing out the restaurant.
They'd feast on saltah and malooga,
sip karkade

and think it apt
that Shibam, with its 16th century high-rise visage
was called the Manhattan of the desert.

Fig juice on fingers and lips, sticky kisses

then on to the excavation,
she'd interrogate the sand with trowels, brushes,
delicately ease out a tickertape of parchment

that her team would fuss over, like midwives
cradling a birth.

Father would watch, growing bored,
wanting only to hold her
into the awe of a UNESCO sunset

but they'd found shattered pottery,
were piecing it into some approximation
of its previous life,

much like I was doing at home
with my mother.

The Inherited Accordion

Squeezing a drone
from its cherry-red body, glazed
like a boiled sweet,

Ryan sits, Guinness'd from the shock
of his Dad's death,
murky-eyed for when *Molly Malone*

would rule the house
and he'd slam his bedroom door,
prefer drum 'n' bass, the occasional Oasis.

The rows: *Get out*
till you can treat your mam and me with respect

so he went
until the funeral's reunion and now
a backlog of jigs and laments

trapped by the ineptitude of fingers;
reeling in the discord
that stalks *The Hills Of Connemara*

where they once walked.

O'Driscoll's at 10

Mock-Gaelic bar, Dublinned
with reproduction black and whites.
It's *where the craic is*
as we knock-back Guinness,
spy a flight of fiddles
nailed to a timbered beam
in the nicotined cumulus.
Wall-mounted bodhrans
suffer the boozed attention
of rhythmically dysfunctional drinkers
preparing for the two-door lottery of *Mna* or *Fir*?
We're all crowded under a Tipperary road sign,
bickering the blame for a bad choice
when the band
resuscitate tin whistles, accordions, tambourines
and we ape Riverdance, clap, kick,
link arms, the circle turning this way, that,
jigging us around, intoxicating,
the unison of the moment, real.

He Works in the Bookshop

so I flick through a Kant
to impress.

On lunch
with the tide in his favour

he walks the causeway,
ignores young women sipping iced tea

on pastel towels. Aloof
as his hair greets the channel breeze.

He settles on rocks,
eats a brie and grape baguette,

watches the seaport
inhaling speedboats to harbour,

puffing out yachts. Doesn't catch
my awkward smile.

Heads back to sell chapter and verse,
leaving me to stew

in the philosophical shallows
of sea and its plethora of fish.

Two Jihadists Sip Water

and discuss tactics
like cold war intellectuals.

In a garden, whispering,
their words cut the heart from America

and her best ever dancing friend.
They've accumulated rucksacks, nails,

ammonium nitrate.
The voices clipped like an English lawn.

A rented garage on the outskirts
keeps tight-lipped

about the stash under tarpaulin.
They're convinced

security forces haven't bugged them
as hydrangeas rear and rustle

over their timings. Confident.
It's the boisterous everydayness

that lets them wait on the platform
next to
        blood types,
                dental work,
                        genetic code.

Fugitives

Twilit mid-west. *Fugitives* she called us,
he'll not find us here. The Dreamliner
slid us out of sky; adventure

for a boy across wheat plains,
our new corrugated home
and my dad, a hundred winds and rains away.

The all-I-have mother opened
and shut our beds, baked bread
while men bullied the land

then she tended the men, beered up,
sweated, on our porch,
her stories loosening heart and wallet,

the slap and groan drowning out crickets,
the distant freight trains.
I rode harvesters

hidden in dust clouds. Never figured
what I'd done wrong. His photos disappeared
like the bruises I couldn't remember.

I wanted to smash Budweisers
into his dwindled face — *he'll not find us here.*
Fourteen years on

I'm hoping she's wrong.

Waterways

The distanced man is you
running with the dog,
your dreadlock hair swishes through mist.
I find your little book of phone numbers
fallen on the towpath,
men's names snarl on every page.

I kneel by the water, set it adrift,
it sinks like an overloaded ferry.
I'll make no mention of the drowned.
From the lock you look back,
wave, smile and later tell me
an optical trick of light and fog and angles

gave you the impression
I was standing on the canal's surface,
deep in concentration
like a delicately floating man.

The Blind Swimmers of East Crumlington

ease naked into the idle river
as they do every 4th of July
when the sun is rowdy with celebration.

The touch of water
like cool silk slipping across their bodies,
hands stroke out,

feet frogging,
they head under the freeway,
smell gasoline, hear a banjo song pour itself

onto the surface
for them to surge through.
They are like salmon, know every eddy

and mud bank. Some upstream boys
on a tire and wood raft
shout abuse, laugh at these eyeless fishmen,

then get snagged on the ribcage
of a sunk-years-ago boat
that spills the mocking cargo

into a thrash and splutter
back to the jetty.
The blind swimmers of East Crumlington

navigate around the wreck,
feel the riverbed's topography
enter them like the Holy Spirit.

They continue
past the old oil refinery,
slicks of skin moving out of sight

to where nobody goes, where nobody knows.

Buddha in the Noodle Bar

You were sure you'd seen him
tucking into a bowl of *Ho Yo Min* and oyster sauce

but apparently none of the other diners
had spotted him or as you surmised,

they were just too polite
to approach for his autograph.

The shopping centre whirrs;
escalators are levitating custom

to emporia
nestling on a plain of faux-marble.

Jewellery reclines on velvet,
baits from behind glass, prices play hard to get.

Clothes shops heat as squeezed youths
swing from hanger to hanger.

I point out Sophie, the girl from *Coffee Mad*,
but you don't see her.

Later we pass by the food hall;
someone is letting their green tea cool

but Buddha is nowhere to be seen,
even though you swear you saw him,

sitting there. Yes, right there in the Noodle Bar.

Simmer Dim

I pull the night over your eyes
but still sun pours in
and birdsong rebounds off your body,

scintillates the chilled air.
We walk across shingle,
consider the horizon

as a tightrope where we balance
over the ghostly cadence of water.
Yes, here we are, wherever light falls

and that is everywhere, our shadows
stretch like elastic
across the voe,

seep into a billion grains of sand;
you and me sealed as tightly as an oyster,
immersed.

You say it's the restless memory of firelight
from Viking pyres that haunt this sky.
It's the Simmer Dim

and we're both convinced
night will never return.

Revelation Walk

What do you think
as you come across crutches
abandoned on the pavement?

You suspect youths;
the rattle and snide of voices
goad their victim,

pinch the trophies,
away at full pelt
before slinging them.

It could be art —
wannabe Emins and Hirsts trying to rile,
your reaction being filmed.

Another thought;
you've just missed the Holy Spirit
park on double yellows,

lure a stranger
and with angels holding traffic wardens back,
administer a miracle of the legs.

You lean the crutches against a wall. Feel
uneasy. Learn how to walk
all over again.

Scuba

Yes I remember.
My body punches into Cornish water.
Falls, loops. I scud
over the bling of anemones,
the armour-plated turtle.

Float with jellyfish blooms
pulsing, untouchable
and those eyes
like exotic fish
in the aquarium of his mask

check on my safety.
I send a thumbs-up
so he flippers on to the other boys,
like a shepherd in shark-sleek wetsuit,
monitoring current and gauge.

Scrawny breezes
sneak into the shower block.
I'm naked as he stands close, soaping,
his hand detours through steam,
wipes lather from my shoulders.

I am always overboard these days,
taking his breath
from the aqualung;
among seaweed beds — pulled one way,
then dragged back. Over and over.

ManRose

digs his soil,
brushes away debris, creosotes long
into the woozy afternoon.

His tiny patch stitched
into a suburban quilt
where regiments of flowers nod in deference.

ManRose (with his eye on the Jones')
casts his pebble to the cordial water
that springs from a garden centre obelisk.

The persistence of privet
takes a clipping down to size.
Sharp lines imposed on borders.

He'll drench aphids in glistening poison
before tea on the decking,
then patrol for chickweed.

A growling Flymo at its master's heel
is ready to deal with dissenting lawn
while pampas grass strokes the furrowed brow.

ManRose withers at dusk,
plants himself in bed
as the moon issues invites

and foxes come out of hiding,
thread through hedges, past wheelie-bins,
their ghostly wildness made welcome.

Son of a Firecracker

She'd leave me in a motel room, toy tipper truck
and a smell of the ocean for company
as she perched on barstools, whispered
sweet Spanish nothings
into the ear of the fattest wallets,

skin the colour of Demerara
for the luckiest man in crocodile shoes,
glowing salsa putting the sunset to shame,
she'd drown her eyes in absinthe
and wait for rescue;

she'd leave me with senor Delgado, who'd croon
to Dean Martin records, show me
the handgun under his bed.
I wished for school
while she was slapping the face

of a good-for-nothing senator,
scarlet bellflower in her lapel, poker
with the boys and when her luck was out
she'd find the moon crushed to powder,
snort its lines and lift back to the heavens;

she'd leave me shaking Tabasco
onto fish from the docks, dogsbody
in Marguerite's restaurant, washing up,
waiting tables, dreaming of girls and pesetas.
El Carnaval,

hair like lava plumes,
outdragging the drag queens, jade stilettos
and a dress slithered around her, they'd samba
along the Avenida de los Santos. She'd love to pout
into the arms of a photographer friend,

beg him to make her a star
as the sky shrieked
with dynamites of colour.
Next morning I trailed through debris,
stepping over dud fireworks

soaked in Camino rain.

Stopped

Karrier van is quiet:
A scrap-yard.
Child ghosts bob up,

look for Mivvis, Orange Maids.
Forgotten,
the sweet teeth of summer

and now nightfall;
Mister Softee
scabs into rust,

paint warps,
headlights ripped out,
wires hang, reach

for the nuts and bolts earth.
One man once,
the enchanter

chiming from his seat,
a creamy alchemy
welcomed at chill point,

fridge now
retired into mould.
Seeped acid,

the battery wallows.
No other vehicle
can ever be this silent.

Flutter

Jack sits on the jetty
along from a swell of motor cruisers,

their chromework flicking light
like the spangle of fruit machines in the bookies.

He wraps a pebble in each betting slip,
drops them to the murk. The surface heals

as if in collusion with someone disposing bodies.
His head is full of injury-time winners, dead-certs,

Alaskan Kiss that fell at the seventh
and his accumulator. The sky darkens,

robbing him of the horizon – stars
find themselves balancing on harbour water.

He knows little about astronomy
but wonders whether Pegasus will appear tonight –

if it were running at Uttoxeter he'd have a punt.
Gulls lull away. Legs dangle, treading air.

Jack sails away
in the reflection of other men's boats.

A Tale at Junction 5

73mph, fast lane,
gantries lost in a downward sun,

your hands working their evasions
on the steering wheel

as a BMW
road-rages alongside, ahead,

tries to run us off the road, veer us
under the tyres

of the largest haulage.
After the gymnastic of expletives

and hand gestures, silence
opens itself out.

I look at your face, a concentrate
of all your abilities and senses;

it reminds me
of our first awkward fuck,

when love took us from where we were
and now

it renews its promise
across the width of the dashboard

while my hand rests on your leg,
bracing for impact.

The Chiropodist's Silhouette

is seen stooping over gloomy feet.
Underneath the fallen arches
her fingers ensnare bunion,
exorcise corn
and pumice into a dust of finished skin.

She teaches toenails the error of their ways,
brings the cracked heel to heal.

Clients leave with spring in sober shoe
while she runs
through the day's takings,
hums a tune from a story heard earlier
of courting, jazz-steps

from times when dances would spill into daylight
and feet never touched the ground.

Emergency Glazier

I'm only in demand when your heavens have blown the day mad. I could never believe your anticyclone, trusting the cry of a Nina Simone say — her pain & blues easily pinned to the wall of my heart, although you could argue anguish in art is not true living. There you go again — glass screams & people shatter, I get it, get you. A little blandishment goes a long way. You want me for my hacking knife, for being putty in your hand & like I say, your cantankerous weather is in love with itself once more, tearing you apart

so let me pick shards from your eyes. I'll fill gaps where the tropics came in. Pain, pane & forecasting. Sealant around the edges, the warping wood. & who said a wet face carries no ripples? Count my devotion in the isobars I've tamed, the bins I've righted. It's all about our clarity & smudges so I'll wipe these windows. This battered house will be a strong house where rooms are windless. I'm many candles wise to your storm-chasing yet still come alive when you need my craft. Dream of tornadoes. Endlessly.

The Confidant's Shadow

He didn't walk out on her when she accused him of having an affair
with the woman next door. He'd only gone round to tame the lawn
but the homemade lemonade said it all.

I took tea with them. They were a lovely couple.
We sat in their cottage garden and ate salmon paste sandwiches.
I felt uncomfortable on the wrought-iron chair and the sun burned.

He didn't leave her when she told him he was a paedophile
after she'd found him watching a BBC holiday programme
where young children splashed the Costas in pools of whooping fun.

We sat in their cottage garden and crunched ginger snaps.
She was as blonde as Cornish ice cream and melted close
to my smile. I sipped tea with them. They were a lovely couple.

He didn't move out after she claimed he was alcoholic,
the empty wine bottle waved under his nose
before star-bursting across flagstone.

I took tea with them. They were a lovely couple.
She had skin as pale as Carrara marble. Her hand brushed my leg.
I felt uncomfortable on the wrought-iron chair and the sun burned.

He didn't desert her when she raged, hair like honeysuckle in a storm.
When she slung his loafers out the window and quoted the Bible,
skimmed a razor across her veins — when their doctor intervened.

They were a lovely couple. I took tea with them. Her eyes were cloudy
with dreams. He stared across the dayroom. I felt uncomfortable
on the fastened plastic chair and the room was airless.

Toilers & Co

Black and white industrial;
terrace ragamuffins all pewter skin and gaslight eyes
lobbing stones at liquorice chimneys.

Canal clogged with cotton fish, coal fish,
the cogs of water turning
and the tar cat washes her tongue

along the street of many puddles,
puddles dispensing views of the gutted, the ferreting,
clothes lines slurred by smog.

Foundry shifts concuss the ear of men,
in hats they pour, hit and bevel the hours away
into a lifetime of iron moons

winched and hanging chain-high
on the oiled backbone of their labour.
Sulphur winds harmonise through tram cables,

the river writhes with turbine fish, piston fish
and everyone knows that pissing on the waterwheel
never made it turn faster,

that it's the speed of gruel soaking
through the other man's bread
that keeps them kissing the grindstone,

longing for horn's blast
to bring their day
to a shuddering-God-almighty-clanking-slam-shut-close.

Whiskers of the tar cat
brush the legs of this black and white industrial.
Its throat full of clinker

to retch at the feet of factory owners
too busy feasting on hog roast,
bloating till their eyes can't open.

Marvel at Her Spa Face

updating under dead sea mud. Days here are tideless. Carrot juice still as a mill-pond. Eyes cucumbered into giving up their bags — unlike her mother who was *unVogue* till the end, with draw-string lips pursed against the fates of the age. A relic from when life was allowed to blast slowly through you & leave the scarring of its malice for all to admire. No time for the frivolity of lipstick, mascara.

Wrapped in seaweed as if prepared for some *nouvelle cuisine* cannibal. The clock is slowing, slow, stopped. Her pores coaxed into giving up toxins. Marine salt scrubs, rubs & tubs — the lavishment of hands, glossy masseurs at work, easing hot basalt stones across her pale terrain, like high-priests attending a Henge ritual. This celestial body is prepared, pre-packaged & when the ghost is pristine Heaven has the catwalk.

Blind Spot

As his tyres before, so feet now,
negotiating the route.
Mindful of drivers
out at this ungodly hour.

He stares; thinks back
to the razor cold.
Late, first week, first job –
foot down along Cheshire lanes,

misjudging the bend
and merging head on
with a woman and her Vauxhall.
She was killed in the time it took

a pheasant to flee the scene.
He remembers nothing of the crash,
only of coming-to in hospital,
being told he almost died.

He's barely considered
whether she had children, a husband,
left grieving parents.
He couldn't care then or now.

This troubles him
as he stands slap-bang
in the middle
of an empty road.

Three-Eyed Wolf

It's the time of the three-eyed wolf.
I don't believe a word of it.
You've got the school children
drawing their excited approximations
and writing warm welcomes
to hang from yard trees.
The forest will stir with wintering curses you say,
grasses bend, stroked by spirits
preparing the way
for the whitest fur to enter the village
and the children are now in bed, gifts left
on porches, by lanterns.
The elders drink moonshine,
scrunch faces over old times,
scratch a fiddle into the small hours
until sleep rounds them up.
We make love on your old mattress,
but your ear is half-tuned
to the hunched night.
You say that to hear his howl
means you have a pure past, an honest present
and a blessed future.
Next morning you're convinced you'd caught
the song of the three-eyed wolf. Life is good.
I'd heard nothing. The legend
curiously real.

The Wreck of the Summer Song

plays its way
through the Beaufort scale, blows in
across this water town, every year

and every year your mouth
looks more like an upturned boat.
You forget the libretto,

forget you nurtured these peonies,
don't recognise your son and daughter,
insist he's just popped inside

for drinks. We wrap you
in your favourite cardigan, your fingers
fumble with buttons,

wayward and pained,
just like they were
when you first learnt the piano.

One of Those Days

when we were knee-deep in the foxglove,
                short-cutting
                        through the old lady's garden,
sun shone backwards,
               pockets full of cash
                         cash
                            cash.
                  Shirts undone.
We were the lone apples:
                  mother's pie, toffee, scrumpy
sore heads,
  grappling with the *mysteries*.
             You'd roll tobacco, ganja, lick the paper shut,
spark up
  out in the grasses
                     or by the shaggy brook
we'd lie down,
          see powerlines like stitches
                holding the sky together.
             Waiting.   We'd wait.
Our faces like twin-decks,   swapping songs,
        Bowie in the ear
             and on the electric wind:
we were young
         and the men were biting.
Newton's apple
              nowhere.

Ballad of Codger

He's coming to the end of himself.
Singing *Gene Vincent*.

Hair like a battleline in retreat.
The doors in his body creak.

He watches a bargain teabag
do its best to bond with water.

   Photograph –

around her like toffee round an apple.
Her breath was mint, was cloves.

   Remembers the crematorium –

the chimney that eased out its reductions,
his wife taking to the sky.

   Get out more –

young men
spruced for the night. He feels deposed

in a pit of lively kings
but likes the echo of the crown.

His mouth like a half-open mussel
glistening by the pool table. Eyeing the talent.

   Half a pint left –

karaoke about to start.
Asks if they have any Vincent.

Checks reflection,
   be bop a lula, she's my baby

The Archetypal Mr. Pisces

points out snowbirds in sacred trees, says
he'll share the mission statement of blizzards,

promises one day we'll burn our algebra
in a motel off some desert highway

in a shower of bourbon
and shamanistic fucking.

He guarantees to modify the circuitry
of my lament, make it as weightless

as a hedgehog's sigh.
At no extra cost he can advise

on how to best position bones
on the windowsill to scare my neighbours.

He challenges me to believe
he can peel an apple on the riverbank

with one hand,
then float his pocketknife on water,

that he could bloody my nose, fatten my lip,
hold me down in the reed beds for a minute and a day

then haul me up beautiful, coughing out poems,
for sure he says, *for sure.*

It's only when we kiss
in the gap between lightning and thunder

that I realise the planets can't help but lie,
why we always fall for it.

Kerosene

It's where crew cut youths jostle

around some worn-down car

& women pick flowers from the roadside

to place on wasteland graves.

The men, skinny as unleavened bread,

you could blindfold

& they'd still catch rabbit in the bare hands

of a dead season. At dusk

they plume with contraband cigar.

Top buttons undone. Kicking stones

through the generator's hum.

It's where we were warned not to go.

They have knives eager for nice boys like us.

Can still hear their gin songs & laughter.

Could point out the kerosene shack

with animal bone hanging above the bed

where he touched my skin all night

& never once used a blade.

flowerheads

florists stand in the layby   backs
bent like late summer stems

& it's another embered sky
long out of rain

some cars stop
inspect the flagging displays   apologies
need to be made

significant dates celebrated   love declared
by way of the petal

soon you'll see the florists
collapse their stalls

air a curse of fume & particulate
filling lungs

you may be driving past   on your way home

trying to remember for the life of you
what type of flower
most appropriate for funerals

Lifer

You told me why you'd murdered her — in your letter;
botched robbery, she was screaming, lashing out, false nail

embedded in your forearm. And you had previous.
My friends wouldn't understand, only one visit

but I knew you were the one, want to lose myself
on your skin, become your most intricate tattoo.

Over the phone swearwords acrobat from your mouth.
You tell me about when you lived at home, your bedroom

with Bruce Lee posters kicking from the walls, you and the boys,
lips taut like scar tissue, Dagenham was yours.

I'm going to wait. Chosen the dress already.
The chain and crucifix — they still smell of your chest.

I keep your letters in a shoe box, under my bed, hidden.
At night I'm frightened mum and dad will hear

as your words punch and punch again,
desperate to get out.

We'll Have No Karaoke Here

where our crumbling houses
meet the flatlands
        and lose their reflection in its mute river,

where there's always a battered Chevrolet
        resting in the dusty wind, radio excised.

Here it is always summer
        in the time of our blues

and we really have no interest
        in how you did it your way, about the men
that came down in droves

        from a generous cloud
to leave their footprints
        on a baked mud road much like your soul.

We'll have no karaoke here;

        the boarded windows of Old Jack's
hold Angels at bay,

        they traipse over smashed glasses,
through disjointing air

        and to put it quite frankly
we don't care one jot about your personal Waterloo
        or why your mama pulled the trigger –

leave our ears as keen as whispering dishes,
        let bar and marquee
bulge with Charts of silence;

        we'll have no karaoke here
to remind us of when we sang in houses of the vinyl dream
        and the mirrors

could only hold their breath.

Acknowledgements

The photograph for the cover image was taken by David Lakin with subsequent artwork by Julia Wernik.

Previous publications (some of which are earlier versions of the poems as they appear in this collection):

- "Bedwetter Stays at The Savoy" was first published in *Orbis* (No. 141 Spring 2007)
- "A Day for the Shakers" was first published in *The London Magazine* (April/May 2005)
- "Winter's Lucky Lady" - Winner of the Playing Bingo Poetry Competition 2013 (Judge – Fawzia Kane) - was first published in *The 1st PlayingBingo.co.uk Anthology of Bingo* (2015)
- "By the Short and Curlies" was first published in *Other Poetry* (Series 2 No. 30 August 2006)
- "The Cherries of Beaufays" was first published in *Brittle Star* (Issue 13 Spring 2006)
- "Old Town Fires" was first published in *Dream Catcher* (Issue 21 April 2008)
- "Windfall" was first published in *Orbis* (No. 161 Autumn 2012)
- "Windchimes" was first published in *Southlight* (Issue 14 - Autumn 2013)
- "Fieldnotes" was first published in *Ambit* (No 211 – Winter 2013)
- "The Inherited Accordion" was first published in *Southlight* (Issue 21 Spring 2017)
- "O'Driscoll's at 10" was first published in *Southlight* (Issue 21 Spring 2017)
- "He Works in the Bookshop" was first published in *The London Magazine* (Aug/Sept 2006)
- "Waterways" was first published in *Brittle Star* (Issue 30 Spring 2012)
- "The Blind Swimmers of East Crumlington" was first published in *Ambit* (No. 211 Winter 2013)
- "Buddha in the Noodle Bar" was first published in *Orbis* (No. 161 Autumn 2012)
- "Simmer Dim" - Highly commended in Yorkshire Open Poetry Competition 2012 (Judge – Neil Rollinson) - was first published in *Stand* (Volume 13 March 2015)
- "Son of a Firecracker" was first published in *The London Magazine* (December/January 2014/15)
- "Stopped" was first published in *South* (Issue 48 – Oct 2013)
- "The Confidant's Shadow" - 4th Place in the Kent & Sussex Open Poetry Competition 2017 (Judge – Catherine Smith) - was first published in *Poetry Folio 71* (Kent & Sussex Poetry Society) (Summer 2017)
- "One of Those Days" was first published in *Poetry Salzburg Review* (No. 29 Spring 2016)
- "Lifer" was first published in *The Interpreter's House* (Issue 61 Feb 2016)

www.ingramcontent.com/pod-product-compliance
Ingram Content Group UK Ltd.
Pitfield, Milton Keynes, MK11 3LW, UK
UKHW020523080325
455946UK00016B/138